THE TRAVELER'S PLAYBOOK:

WORLD EDITION

Designed with 💚 and inspiration from around the world.

The Traveler's Playbook: World Edition

Copyright © Deanna Didzun, 2021

All rights reserved. No part of this book may be used or reproduced in any manner whatsoever without written permission from the author, except in the case of reprints in the context of reviews.

Second Edition, 2021
ISBN: 978-0-578-97575-7

The Traveler's Playbook
www.thetravelersplaybook.com
IG Hashtag: #thetravelersplaybook

Book & Cover Design: Brianna Showalter, Ruston, WA
Printed in Canada.

The Traveler's Playbook is available at quantity discounts with bulk purchase. For more information, please e-mail hello@thetravelersplaybook.com

Why Pack
The Traveler's Playbook?

• • • • • • • • • • • •

Dear World Traveler,

I am so glad my Playbook found you! Whether you are planning your first trip or have been around the world already, I hope this world travel journal will help you record your fondest memories and create the ultimate souvenir!

Each country has its own dedicated page with easy to follow prompts that cover fun details from your trip. Make sure you explore the Playbook beginning to end as I have included some other fun pages!

The guidance and direction throughout the Playbook should make it as easy as possible to use, but remember, this is YOUR Playbook and you should include whatever shows off you and your adventures best.

Bon Voyage!
-Deanna

Inspiration Board

Include anything
(quotes, images,
photos) that
inspires
your travel.

The Adventures of:

Name:

Nationality:

Phone Number:

Email Address:

Finder's Fee:

The Ultimate

☐ Made It!

☐ Totally Worth It!

☐ AMAZING!

☐ Check!

☐ A Dream Come True!

Add a **place** from your bucket list in each banner
Then mark each off

Bucket List

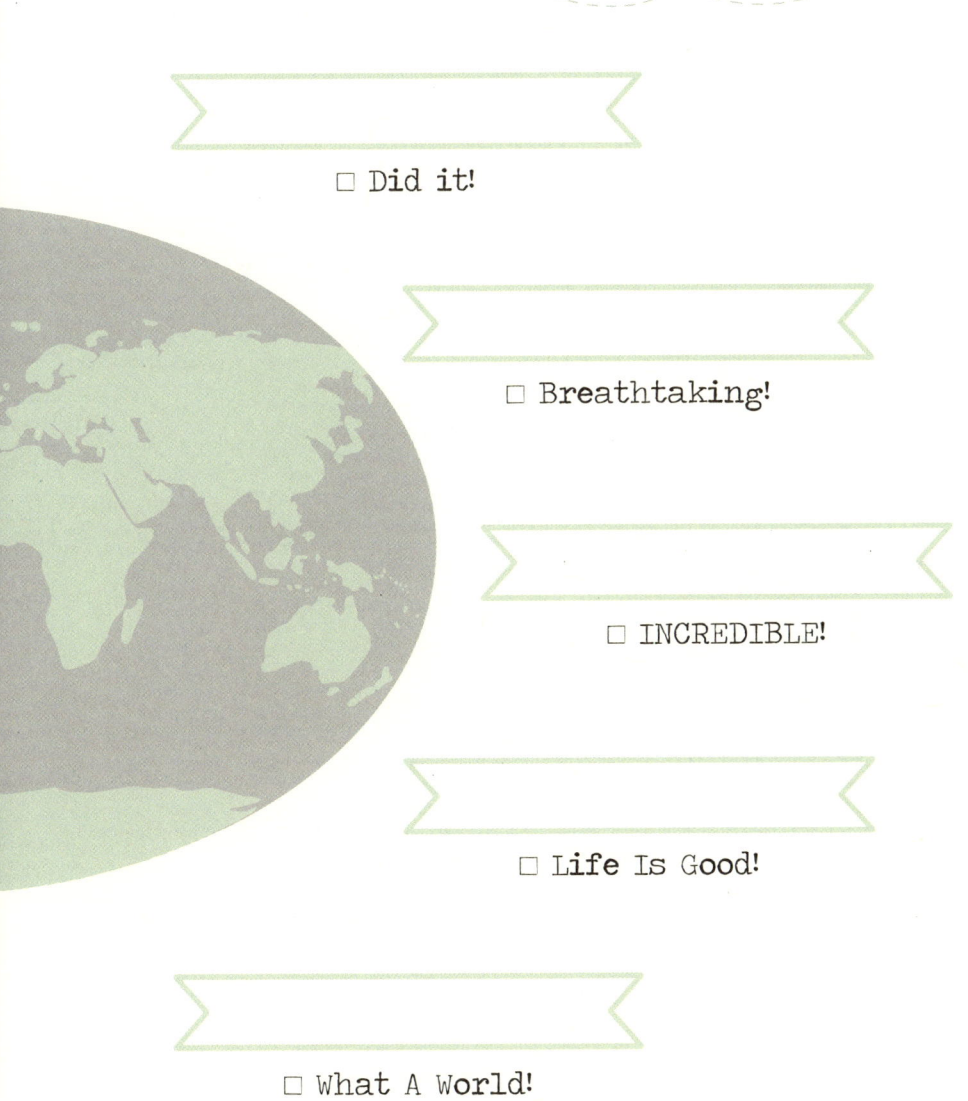

☐ Did it!

☐ Breathtaking!

☐ INCREDIBLE!

☐ Life Is Good!

☐ What A World!

and draw a line to its location on the globe.
as you complete it!

 # Check Out

AFRICA

- Algeria
- Angola
- Benin
- Botswana
- Burkina Faso
- Burundi
- Cabo Verde
- Cameroon
- Central African Republic
- Chad
- Comoros
- Democratic Republic of the Congo
- Republic of the Congo
- Côte d'Ivoire
- Djibouti
- Egypt
- Equatorial Guinea
- Eritrea
- Eswatini
- Ethiopia
- Gabon
- The Gambia
- Ghana
- Guinea
- Guinea-Bissau
- Kenya
- Lesotho
- Liberia
- Libya
- Madagascar
- Malawi
- Mali
- Mauritania
- Mauritius
- Morocco
- Mozambique
- Namibia
- Niger
- Nigeria
- Rwanda
- São Tomé and Príncipe
- Senegal
- Seychelles
- Sierra Leone
- Somalia
- South Africa
- South Sudan
- Sudan
- Tanzania
- Togo
- Tunisia
- Uganda
- Zambia
- Zimbabwe

ASIA

- Afghanistan
- Armenia
- Azerbaijan
- Bahrain
- Bangladesh
- Bhutan
- Brunei
- Cambodia
- China
- Cyprus
- Georgia
- India
- Indonesia
- Iran
- Iraq
- Israel
- Japan
- Jordan
- Kazakhstan
- Kuwait
- Kyrgyzstan
- Laos
- Lebanon
- Malaysia
- Maldives
- Mongolia
- Myanmar
- Nepal
- North Korea
- Oman
- Pakistan
- Palestine
- Philippines
- Qatar
- Russia
- Saudi Arabia
- Singapore
- South Korea
- Sri Lanka
- Syria
- Taiwan
- Tajikistan
- Thailand
- Timor-Leste
- Turkey
- Turkmenistan
- United Arab Emirates
- Uzbekistan
- Vietnam
- Yemen

Where I've Been!

EUROPE

- ☐ Albania
- ☐ Andorra
- ☐ Austria
- ☐ Belarus
- ☐ Belgium
- ☐ Bosnia and Herzegovina
- ☐ Bulgaria
- ☐ Croatia
- ☐ Czech Republic
- ☐ Denmark
- ☐ England
- ☐ Estonia
- ☐ Finland
- ☐ France
- ☐ Germany
- ☐ Greece
- ☐ Hungary
- ☐ Iceland
- ☐ Northern Ireland
- ☐ Republic of Ireland
- ☐ Italy
- ☐ Kosovo
- ☐ Latvia
- ☐ Liechtenstein
- ☐ Lithuania
- ☐ Luxembourg
- ☐ Malta
- ☐ Moldova
- ☐ Monaco
- ☐ Montenegro
- ☐ Netherlands
- ☐ North Macedonia
- ☐ Norway
- ☐ Poland
- ☐ Portugal
- ☐ Romania
- ☐ San Marino
- ☐ Scotland
- ☐ Serbia
- ☐ Slovakia
- ☐ Slovenia
- ☐ Spain
- ☐ Sweden
- ☐ Switzerland
- ☐ Ukraine
- ☐ Vatican City
- ☐ Wales

NORTH AMERICA

- ☐ Antigua and Barbuda
- ☐ The Bahamas
- ☐ Barbados
- ☐ Belize
- ☐ Canada
- ☐ Costa Rica
- ☐ Cuba
- ☐ Dominica
- ☐ Dominican Republic
- ☐ El Salvador
- ☐ Grenada
- ☐ Guatemala
- ☐ Haiti
- ☐ Honduras
- ☐ Jamaica
- ☐ Mexico
- ☐ Nicaragua
- ☐ Panama
- ☐ Saint Kitts and Nevis
- ☐ Saint Lucia
- ☐ Saint Vincent and the Grenadines
- ☐ Trinidad and Tobago
- ☐ United States of America

OCEANIA

- ☐ Australia
- ☐ Fiji
- ☐ Kiribati
- ☐ Marshall Islands
- ☐ Federated States of Micronesia
- ☐ Nauru
- ☐ New Zealand
- ☐ Palau
- ☐ Papua New Guinea
- ☐ Samoa
- ☐ Solomon Islands
- ☐ Tonga
- ☐ Tuvalu
- ☐ Vanuatu

SOUTH AMERICA

- ☐ Argentina
- ☐ Bolivia
- ☐ Brazil
- ☐ Chile
- ☐ Colombia
- ☐ Ecuador
- ☐ Guyana
- ☐ Paraguay
- ☐ Peru
- ☐ Suriname
- ☐ Uruguay
- ☐ Venezuela

★BONUS: ☐ Antarctica

My Journey

(Antarctica)

In Color

Color in the countries you have visited!

List the places you visit (and when) in order, creating a tally and timeline all in one!

Master Journey Tracker

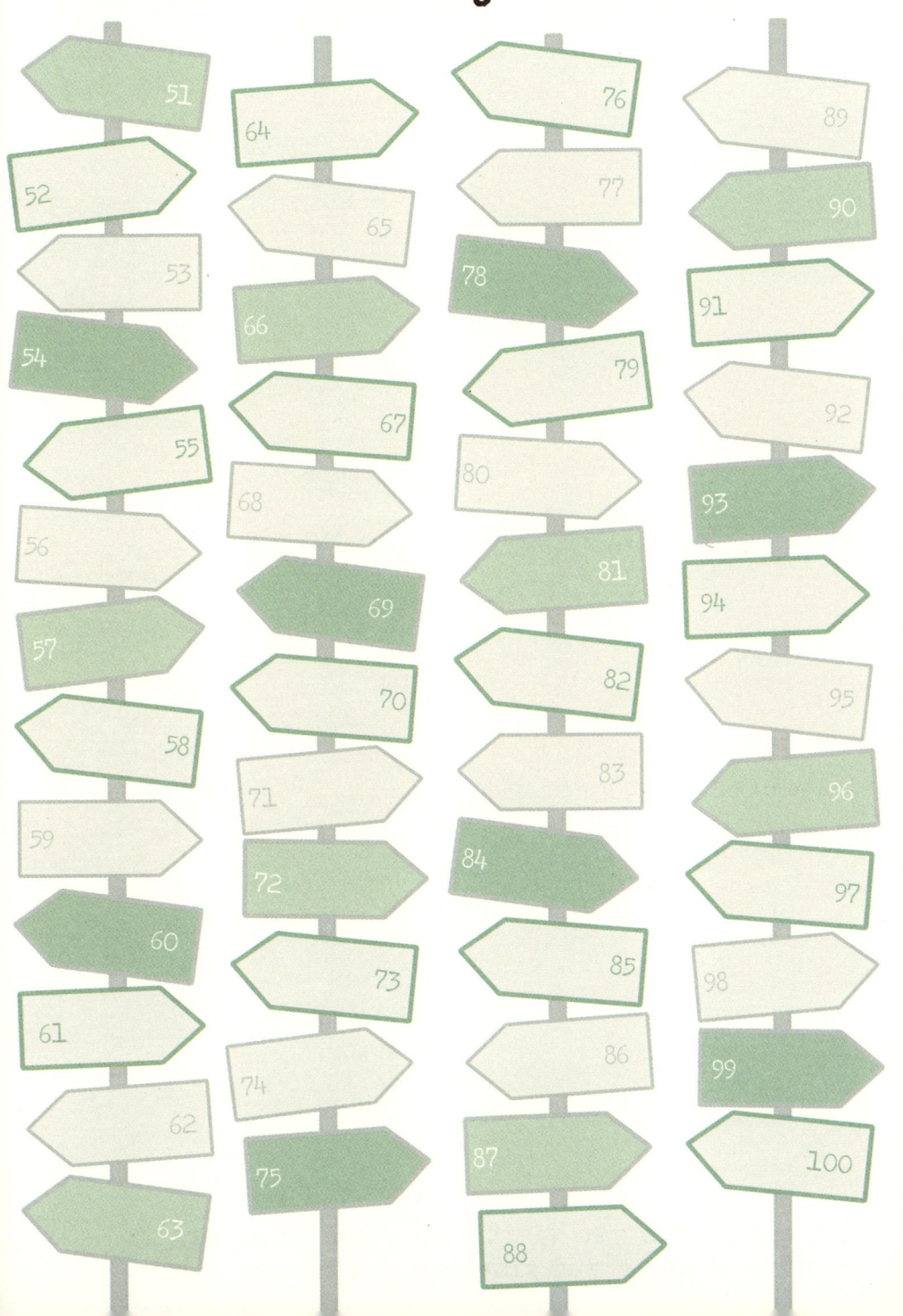

Photos & Keepsakes From...

Draw your best version of the country's flag.

Algeria

List 4 places you visited and rate them by coloring in one to five stars (☆).

Dates
Arrive | Depart

Food & Drinks

Sights

☆☆☆☆☆
☆☆☆☆☆
☆☆☆☆☆
☆☆☆☆☆

Cities

○   ○
○   ○

List the cities you explored around the country!

Frame fits a wallet sized photo and don't forget to include a caption below.

Memories

OVERALL RATING: /5

Angola

Dates
Arrive | Depart

Sights
☆☆☆☆☆
☆☆☆☆☆
☆☆☆☆☆
☆☆☆☆☆

Food & Drinks

Cities
○ ○
○ ○

Memories

OVERALL RATING: /5

Benin

Dates
Arrive | Depart

Food & Drinks

Sights
☆☆☆☆☆
☆☆☆☆☆
☆☆☆☆☆
☆☆☆☆☆

Cities
○   ○
○   ○

Memories

OVERALL RATING: /5

Botswana

Dates
Arrive | Depart

Sights
☆☆☆☆☆
☆☆☆☆☆
☆☆☆☆☆
☆☆☆☆☆

Food & Drinks

Cities
○ ○
○ ○

Memories

OVERALL RATING: /5

Burkina Faso

Dates
Arrive | Depart

Food & Drinks

Sights
☆☆☆☆☆
☆☆☆☆☆
☆☆☆☆☆
☆☆☆☆☆

Cities
○ ○
○ ○

Memories

OVERALL RATING: /5

Burundi

Dates
Arrive | Depart

Sights
☆☆☆☆☆
☆☆☆☆☆
☆☆☆☆☆
☆☆☆☆☆

Cities
○　　　○
○　　　○

Food & Drinks

Memories

OVERALL RATING: /5

Cabo Verde

Dates
Arrive | Depart

Sights
☆☆☆☆☆
☆☆☆☆☆
☆☆☆☆☆
☆☆☆☆☆

Food & Drinks

Cities
○　　　○
○　　　○

Memories

OVERALL RATING: /5

Cameroon

Dates
Arrive | Depart

Sights
☆☆☆☆☆
☆☆☆☆☆
☆☆☆☆☆
☆☆☆☆☆

Cities
○　　○
○　　○

Food & Drinks

Memories

OVERALL RATING: /5

Central African Republic

Dates
Arrive | Depart

Sights
☆☆☆☆☆
☆☆☆☆☆
☆☆☆☆☆
☆☆☆☆☆

Cities
○ ○
○ ○

Memories

OVERALL RATING: /5

Chad

Dates
Arrive | Depart

Sights
☆☆☆☆☆
☆☆☆☆☆
☆☆☆☆☆
☆☆☆☆☆

Food & Drinks

Cities
○　　○
○　　○

Memories

OVERALL RATING: /5

Comoros

Dates
Arrive | Depart

Sights
☆☆☆☆☆
☆☆☆☆☆
☆☆☆☆☆
☆☆☆☆☆

Cities
○ ○
○ ○

Memories

OVERALL RATING: /5

Democratic Republic of the Congo

Dates
Arrive | Depart

Sights
☆☆☆☆☆
☆☆☆☆☆
☆☆☆☆☆
☆☆☆☆☆

Food & Drinks

Cities
○ ○
○ ○

Memories

OVERALL RATING: /5

Republic of the Congo

Dates
Arrive	Depart

Sights
☆☆☆☆☆
☆☆☆☆☆
☆☆☆☆☆
☆☆☆☆☆

Food & Drinks

Cities
-
-
-
-

Memories

OVERALL RATING: /5

Côte d'Ivoire

Dates
Arrive | Depart

Sights
☆☆☆☆☆
☆☆☆☆☆
☆☆☆☆☆
☆☆☆☆☆

Food & Drinks

Cities
○　　　○
○　　　○

Memories

OVERALL RATING: /5

Djibouti

Dates
Arrive	Depart

Food & Drinks

Sights
☆☆☆☆☆
☆☆☆☆☆
☆☆☆☆☆
☆☆☆☆☆

Cities
○ ○
○ ○

Memories

OVERALL RATING: /5

Egypt

Dates
Arrive | Depart

Sights
☆☆☆☆☆
☆☆☆☆☆
☆☆☆☆☆
☆☆☆☆☆

Food & Drinks

Cities
○ ○
○ ○

Memories

OVERALL RATING: /5

Equatorial Guinea

Dates
Arrive	Depart

Sights
☆☆☆☆☆
☆☆☆☆☆
☆☆☆☆☆
☆☆☆☆☆

Food & Drinks

Cities
○　　　○
○　　　○

Memories

OVERALL RATING: /5

Eritrea

Dates
Arrive | Depart

Sights
☆☆☆☆☆
☆☆☆☆☆
☆☆☆☆☆
☆☆☆☆☆

Food & Drinks

Cities
○   ○
○   ○

Memories

OVERALL RATING: /5

Eswatini

Dates
Arrive | Depart

Food & Drinks

Sights

☆☆☆☆☆
☆☆☆☆☆
☆☆☆☆☆
☆☆☆☆☆

Cities

○　　○
○　　○

Memories

OVERALL RATING: /5

Ethiopia

Dates
Arrive | Depart

Sights
☆☆☆☆☆
☆☆☆☆☆
☆☆☆☆☆
☆☆☆☆☆

Food & Drinks

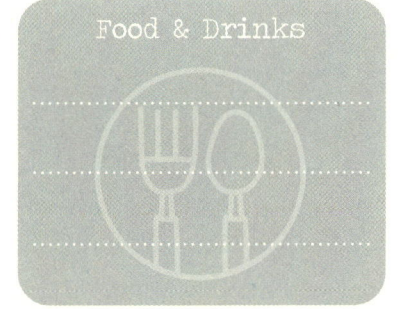

Cities
○ ○
○ ○

Memories

OVERALL RATING: /5

Gabon

Dates
Arrive | Depart

Sights
☆☆☆☆☆
☆☆☆☆☆
☆☆☆☆☆
☆☆☆☆☆

Food & Drinks

Cities
○　　　○
○　　　○

Memories

OVERALL RATING: /5

The Gambia

Dates
Arrive | Depart

Sights
☆☆☆☆☆
☆☆☆☆☆
☆☆☆☆☆
☆☆☆☆☆

Cities
○ ○
○ ○

Food & Drinks

Memories

OVERALL RATING: /5

Ghana

Dates
Arrive | Depart

Sights
☆☆☆☆☆
☆☆☆☆☆
☆☆☆☆☆
☆☆☆☆☆

Cities
○ ○
○ ○

Memories

OVERALL RATING: /5

Guinea

Dates
Arrive	Depart

Sights
☆☆☆☆☆
☆☆☆☆☆
☆☆☆☆☆
☆☆☆☆☆

Food & Drinks

Cities
○
○
○
○

Memories

OVERALL RATING: /5

Guinea-Bissau

Dates
Arrive | Depart

Sights
☆☆☆☆☆
☆☆☆☆☆
☆☆☆☆☆
☆☆☆☆☆

Cities
○　　　○
○　　　○

Food & Drinks

Memories

OVERALL RATING: /5

Kenya

Dates
Arrive | Depart

Sights
☆☆☆☆☆
☆☆☆☆☆
☆☆☆☆☆
☆☆☆☆☆

Food & Drinks

Cities
○ ○
○ ○

Memories

OVERALL RATING: /5

Lesotho

Dates
Arrive | Depart

Sights
☆☆☆☆☆
☆☆☆☆☆
☆☆☆☆☆
☆☆☆☆☆

Food & Drinks

Cities
○ ○
○ ○

Memories

OVERALL RATING: /5

Liberia

Dates
Arrive | Depart

Sights
☆☆☆☆☆
☆☆☆☆☆
☆☆☆☆☆
☆☆☆☆☆

Food & Drinks

Cities
○   ○
○   ○

Memories

OVERALL RATING: /5

Libya

Dates
Arrive | Depart

Sights
☆☆☆☆☆
☆☆☆☆☆
☆☆☆☆☆
☆☆☆☆☆

Food & Drinks

Cities
○　　　○
○　　　○

Memories

OVERALL RATING: /5

Madagascar

Dates
Arrive | Depart

Sights
☆☆☆☆☆
☆☆☆☆☆
☆☆☆☆☆
☆☆☆☆☆

Food & Drinks

Cities
○ ○
○ ○

Memories

OVERALL RATING: /5

Malawi

Dates
Arrive | Depart

Sights
☆☆☆☆☆
☆☆☆☆☆
☆☆☆☆☆
☆☆☆☆☆

Food & Drinks

Cities
○   ○
○   ○

Memories

OVERALL RATING: /5

Mali

Dates
Arrive | Depart

Sights
☆☆☆☆☆
☆☆☆☆☆
☆☆☆☆☆
☆☆☆☆☆

Food & Drinks

Cities
○ ○
○ ○

Memories

OVERALL RATING: /5

Mauritania

Dates
Arrive | Depart

Sights
☆☆☆☆☆
☆☆☆☆☆
☆☆☆☆☆
☆☆☆☆☆

Food & Drinks

Cities
○ ○
○ ○

Memories

OVERALL RATING: /5

Mauritius

Dates
Arrive | Depart

Sights
☆☆☆☆☆
☆☆☆☆☆
☆☆☆☆☆
☆☆☆☆☆

Food & Drinks

Cities
○ ○
○ ○

Memories

OVERALL RATING: /5

Morocco

Dates
Arrive | Depart

Sights
☆☆☆☆☆
☆☆☆☆☆
☆☆☆☆☆
☆☆☆☆☆

Food & Drinks

Cities
○   ○
○   ○

Memories

OVERALL RATING: /5

Mozambique

Dates
Arrive | Depart

Sights
☆☆☆☆☆
☆☆☆☆☆
☆☆☆☆☆
☆☆☆☆☆

Cities
○ ○
○ ○

Food & Drinks

Memories

OVERALL RATING: /5

Namibia

Dates
Arrive | Depart

Sights
☆☆☆☆☆
☆☆☆☆☆
☆☆☆☆☆
☆☆☆☆☆

Food & Drinks

Cities
○   ○
○   ○

Memories

OVERALL RATING: /5

Niger

Dates
Arrive   Depart

Sights
☆☆☆☆☆
☆☆☆☆☆
☆☆☆☆☆
☆☆☆☆☆

Cities
○　　　○
○　　　○

Food & Drinks

Memories

OVERALL RATING: /5

Nigeria

Dates
Arrive | Depart

Food & Drinks

Sights
☆☆☆☆☆
☆☆☆☆☆
☆☆☆☆☆
☆☆☆☆☆

Cities
○　　　○
○　　　○

Memories

OVERALL RATING: /5

Rwanda

Dates
Arrive | Depart

Food & Drinks

Sights
☆☆☆☆☆
☆☆☆☆☆
☆☆☆☆☆
☆☆☆☆☆

Cities
○   ○
○   ○

Memories

OVERALL RATING: /5

São Tomé and Príncipe

Dates
Arrive | Depart

Sights
☆☆☆☆☆
☆☆☆☆☆
☆☆☆☆☆
☆☆☆☆☆

Food & Drinks

Cities

Memories

OVERALL RATING: /5

Senegal

Dates
Arrive | Depart

Sights
☆☆☆☆☆
☆☆☆☆☆
☆☆☆☆☆
☆☆☆☆☆

Food & Drinks

Cities
○   ○
○   ○

Memories

OVERALL RATING: /5

Seychelles

Dates
Arrive | Depart

Sights
☆☆☆☆☆
☆☆☆☆☆
☆☆☆☆☆
☆☆☆☆☆

Food & Drinks

Cities
○   ○
○   ○

Memories

OVERALL RATING: /5

Sierra Leone

Dates
Arrive | Depart

Sights
☆☆☆☆☆
☆☆☆☆☆
☆☆☆☆☆
☆☆☆☆☆

Cities
○
○
○
○

Food & Drinks

Memories

OVERALL RATING: /5

Somalia

Dates
Arrive | Depart

Sights
☆☆☆☆☆
☆☆☆☆☆
☆☆☆☆☆
☆☆☆☆☆

Food & Drinks

Cities
○ ○
○ ○

Memories

OVERALL RATING: /5

South Africa

Dates
Arrive | Depart

Sights
☆☆☆☆☆
☆☆☆☆☆
☆☆☆☆☆
☆☆☆☆☆

Food & Drinks

Cities
○ ○
○ ○

Memories

OVERALL RATING: /5

South Sudan

Dates
Arrive	Depart

Sights
☆☆☆☆☆
☆☆☆☆☆
☆☆☆☆☆
☆☆☆☆☆

Food & Drinks

Cities
○ ○
○ ○

Memories

OVERALL RATING: /5

Sudan

Dates
Arrive | Depart

Sights

Food & Drinks

Cities

Memories

OVERALL RATING: /5

Tanzania

Dates
Arrive	Depart

Sights
☆☆☆☆☆
☆☆☆☆☆
☆☆☆☆☆
☆☆☆☆☆

Food & Drinks

Cities
○   ○
○   ○

Memories

OVERALL RATING: /5

Togo

Dates
Arrive | Depart

Sights
☆☆☆☆☆
☆☆☆☆☆
☆☆☆☆☆
☆☆☆☆☆

Food & Drinks

Cities
○
○
○
○

Memories

OVERALL RATING: /5

Tunisia

Dates
Arrive	Depart

Sights
☆☆☆☆☆
☆☆☆☆☆
☆☆☆☆☆
☆☆☆☆☆

Food & Drinks

Cities
○   ○
○   ○

Memories

OVERALL RATING: /5

Uganda

Dates
Arrive	Depart

Sights
☆☆☆☆☆
☆☆☆☆☆
☆☆☆☆☆
☆☆☆☆☆

Food & Drinks

Cities
○   ○
○   ○

Memories

OVERALL RATING: /5

Zambia

Dates
Arrive | Depart

Sights
☆☆☆☆☆
☆☆☆☆☆
☆☆☆☆☆
☆☆☆☆☆

Food & Drinks

Cities
○   ○
○   ○

Memories

OVERALL RATING: /5

Zimbabwe

Dates
Arrive | Depart

Sights
☆☆☆☆☆
☆☆☆☆☆
☆☆☆☆☆
☆☆☆☆☆

Food & Drinks

Cities
○ ○
○ ○

Memories

OVERALL RATING: /5

My Favorites

- Market
  - Location
- Tour
  - Location
- Food
  - Location
- I Learned
- Strangest Experience

From AFRICA

- Animal
- Location
- Beach
- Location
- Souvenir
- Location
- Must Do
- Funniest Moment

Photos & Keepsakes From...

ASIA

Draw your best version of the country's flag.

Afghanistan

List 4 places you visited and rate them by coloring in one to five stars (☆).

Dates
Arrive | Depart

Sights
☆☆☆☆☆
☆☆☆☆☆
☆☆☆☆☆
☆☆☆☆☆

Food & Drinks

Cities
○ ○
○ ○

List the cities you explored around the country!

Frame fits a wallet sized photo and don't forget to include a caption below.

Memories

OVERALL RATING: /5

Armenia

Dates
Arrive | Depart

Sights
☆☆☆☆☆
☆☆☆☆☆
☆☆☆☆☆
☆☆☆☆☆

Cities
○   ○
○   ○

Food & Drinks

Memories

OVERALL RATING: /5

Azerbaijan

Dates
Arrive | Depart

Sights
☆☆☆☆☆
☆☆☆☆☆
☆☆☆☆☆
☆☆☆☆☆

Food & Drinks

Cities
○   ○
○   ○

Memories

OVERALL RATING: /5

Bahrain

Dates
Arrive | Depart

Sights
☆☆☆☆☆
☆☆☆☆☆
☆☆☆☆☆
☆☆☆☆☆

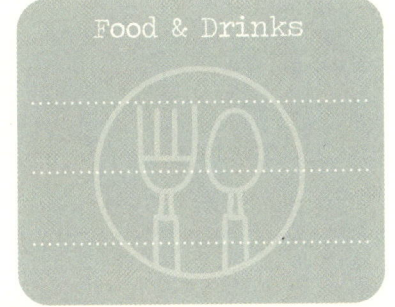

Cities
○　　○
○　　○

Memories

OVERALL RATING: /5

Bangladesh

Dates
Arrive | Depart

Sights
☆☆☆☆☆
☆☆☆☆☆
☆☆☆☆☆
☆☆☆☆☆

Cities
○
○
○
○

Food & Drinks

Memories

OVERALL RATING: /5

Bhutan

Dates
Arrive | Depart

Sights
☆☆☆☆☆
☆☆☆☆☆
☆☆☆☆☆
☆☆☆☆☆

Cities

Food & Drinks

Memories

OVERALL RATING: /5

Brunei

Dates
Arrive | Depart

Sights

Food & Drinks

Cities
○ ○
○ ○

Memories

OVERALL RATING: /5

Cambodia

Dates
Arrive | Depart

Sights
☆☆☆☆☆
☆☆☆☆☆
☆☆☆☆☆
☆☆☆☆☆

Food & Drinks

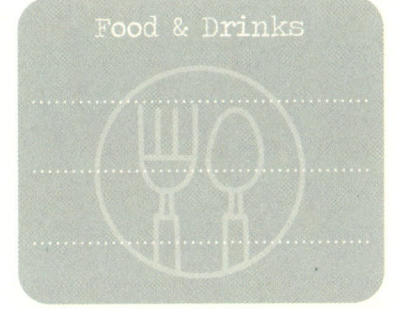

Cities
○ ○
○ ○

Memories

OVERALL RATING: /5

China

Dates
Arrive | Depart

Sights
☆☆☆☆☆
☆☆☆☆☆
☆☆☆☆☆
☆☆☆☆☆

Cities
○ ○
○ ○

Memories

OVERALL RATING: /5

Cyprus

Dates
Arrive | Depart

Sights
☆☆☆☆☆
☆☆☆☆☆
☆☆☆☆☆
☆☆☆☆☆

Cities
○   ○
○   ○

Food & Drinks

Memories

OVERALL RATING: /5

Georgia

Dates
Arrive	Depart

Sights
☆☆☆☆☆
☆☆☆☆☆
☆☆☆☆☆
☆☆☆☆☆

Food & Drinks

Cities
○   ○
○   ○

Memories

OVERALL RATING: /5

India

Dates
Arrive | Depart

Sights
☆☆☆☆☆
☆☆☆☆☆
☆☆☆☆☆
☆☆☆☆☆

Food & Drinks

Cities
○　　　○
○　　　○

Memories

OVERALL RATING: /5

Indonesia

Dates
Arrive | Depart

Food & Drinks

Sights

Cities
○ ○
○ ○

Memories

OVERALL RATING: /5

Iran

Dates
Arrive | Depart

Sights
☆☆☆☆☆
☆☆☆☆☆
☆☆☆☆☆
☆☆☆☆☆

Food & Drinks

Cities
○ ○
○ ○

Memories

OVERALL RATING: /5

Iraq

Dates
Arrive | Depart

Sights
☆☆☆☆☆
☆☆☆☆☆
☆☆☆☆☆
☆☆☆☆☆

Cities
○　　○
○　　○

Food & Drinks

Memories

OVERALL RATING: /5

Israel

Dates
Arrive | Depart

Sights
☆☆☆☆☆
☆☆☆☆☆
☆☆☆☆☆
☆☆☆☆☆

Cities
○ ○
○ ○

Food & Drinks

Memories

OVERALL RATING: /5

Japan

Dates
Arrive | Depart

Sights
☆☆☆☆☆
☆☆☆☆☆
☆☆☆☆☆
☆☆☆☆☆

Cities
○ ○
○ ○

Food & Drinks

Memories

OVERALL RATING: /5

Jordan

Dates
Arrive | Depart

Sights
☆☆☆☆☆
☆☆☆☆☆
☆☆☆☆☆
☆☆☆☆☆

Food & Drinks

Cities
○ ○
○ ○

Memories

OVERALL RATING: /5

Kazakhstan

Dates
Arrive	Depart

Food & Drinks

Sights
☆☆☆☆☆
☆☆☆☆☆
☆☆☆☆☆
☆☆☆☆☆

Cities
○ ○
○ ○

Memories

OVERALL RATING: /5

Kuwait

Dates
Arrive | Depart

Sights
☆☆☆☆☆
☆☆☆☆☆
☆☆☆☆☆
☆☆☆☆☆

Food & Drinks

Cities
○   ○
○   ○

Memories

OVERALL RATING: /5

Kyrgyzstan

Dates
Arrive | Depart

Sights
☆☆☆☆☆
☆☆☆☆☆
☆☆☆☆☆
☆☆☆☆☆

Food & Drinks

Cities
○   ○
○   ○

Memories

OVERALL RATING: /5

Laos

Dates
Arrive | Depart

Sights
☆☆☆☆☆
☆☆☆☆☆
☆☆☆☆☆
☆☆☆☆☆

Cities
○　　　○
○　　　○

Food & Drinks

Memories

OVERALL RATING: /5

Lebanon

Dates
Arrive	Depart

Sights
☆☆☆☆☆
☆☆☆☆☆
☆☆☆☆☆
☆☆☆☆☆

Food & Drinks

Cities
○ ○
○ ○

Memories

OVERALL RATING: /5

Malaysia

Dates
Arrive | Depart

Sights
☆☆☆☆☆
☆☆☆☆☆
☆☆☆☆☆
☆☆☆☆☆

Food & Drinks

Cities
○ ○
○ ○

Memories

OVERALL RATING: /5

Maldives

Dates
Arrive	Depart

Food & Drinks

Sights

☆☆☆☆☆
☆☆☆☆☆
☆☆☆☆☆
☆☆☆☆☆

Cities
○   ○
○   ○

Memories

OVERALL RATING: /5

Mongolia

Dates
Arrive | Depart

Sights
☆☆☆☆☆
☆☆☆☆☆
☆☆☆☆☆
☆☆☆☆☆

Food & Drinks

Cities
○ ○
○ ○

Memories

OVERALL RATING: /5

Myanmar

Dates
Arrive | Depart

Sights
☆☆☆☆☆
☆☆☆☆☆
☆☆☆☆☆
☆☆☆☆☆

Cities
○   ○
○   ○

Food & Drinks

Memories

OVERALL RATING: /5

(The world's only non-quadrilateral flag!)

Nepal

Dates
Arrive | Depart

Sights
☆☆☆☆☆
☆☆☆☆☆
☆☆☆☆☆
☆☆☆☆☆

Cities
○　　○
○　　○

Memories

OVERALL RATING: /5

North Korea

Dates
Arrive | Depart

Sights
☆☆☆☆☆
☆☆☆☆☆
☆☆☆☆☆
☆☆☆☆☆

Food & Drinks

Cities
○　　○
○　　○

Memories

OVERALL RATING: /5

Oman

Dates
Arrive | Depart

Sights
☆☆☆☆☆
☆☆☆☆☆
☆☆☆☆☆
☆☆☆☆☆

Food & Drinks

Cities
○ ○
○ ○

Memories

OVERALL RATING: /5

Pakistan

Dates
Arrive | Depart

Sights
☆☆☆☆☆
☆☆☆☆☆
☆☆☆☆☆
☆☆☆☆☆

Cities
○ ○
○ ○

Food & Drinks

Memories

OVERALL RATING: /5

Palestine

Dates
Arrive | Depart

Sights
☆☆☆☆☆
☆☆☆☆☆
☆☆☆☆☆
☆☆☆☆☆

Cities
○　　　○
○　　　○

Memories

OVERALL RATING: /5

Philippines

Dates
Arrive | Depart

Sights
☆☆☆☆☆
☆☆☆☆☆
☆☆☆☆☆
☆☆☆☆☆

Cities
○　　　○
○　　　○

Food & Drinks

Memories

OVERALL RATING: /5

Qatar

Dates
Arrive | Depart

Food & Drinks

Sights
☆☆☆☆☆
☆☆☆☆☆
☆☆☆☆☆
☆☆☆☆☆

Cities
○   ○
○   ○

Memories

OVERALL RATING: /5

Russia

Dates
Arrive | Depart

Sights
☆☆☆☆☆
☆☆☆☆☆
☆☆☆☆☆
☆☆☆☆☆

Cities
○　　　○
○　　　○

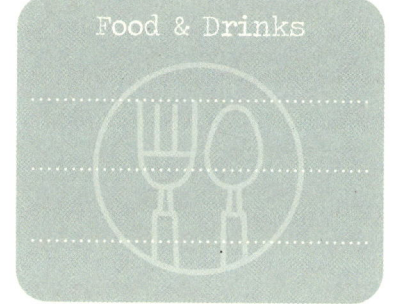

Food & Drinks

Memories

OVERALL RATING:　/5

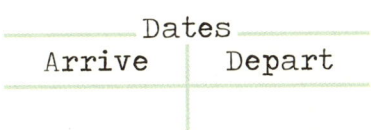

Saudi Arabia

Dates
Arrive | Depart

Sights
☆☆☆☆☆
☆☆☆☆☆
☆☆☆☆☆
☆☆☆☆☆

Cities
○   ○
○   ○

Food & Drinks

Memories

OVERALL RATING: /5

Singapore

Dates
Arrive | Depart

Food & Drinks

Sights
☆☆☆☆☆
☆☆☆☆☆
☆☆☆☆☆
☆☆☆☆☆

Cities
○ ○
○ ○

Memories

OVERALL RATING: /5

South Korea

Dates
Arrive | Depart

Sights
☆☆☆☆☆
☆☆☆☆☆
☆☆☆☆☆
☆☆☆☆☆

Cities
○　　　○
○　　　○

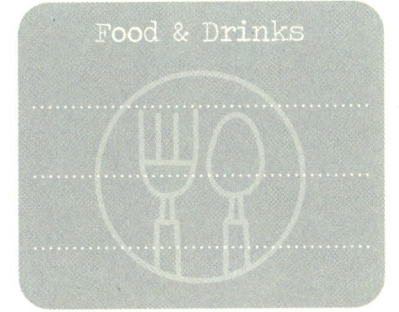
Food & Drinks

Memories

OVERALL RATING: /5

Sri Lanka

Dates
Arrive Depart

Food & Drinks

Sights
☆☆☆☆☆
☆☆☆☆☆
☆☆☆☆☆
☆☆☆☆☆

Cities
○　　　○
○　　　○

Memories

OVERALL RATING: /5

Syria

Dates
Arrive | Depart

Sights
☆☆☆☆☆
☆☆☆☆☆
☆☆☆☆☆
☆☆☆☆☆

Cities
○ ○
○ ○

Memories

OVERALL RATING: /5

Taiwan

Dates
Arrive | Depart

Sights
☆☆☆☆☆
☆☆☆☆☆
☆☆☆☆☆
☆☆☆☆☆

Food & Drinks

Cities
○ ○
○ ○

Memories

OVERALL RATING: /5

Tajikistan

Dates
Arrive | Depart

Sights
☆☆☆☆☆
☆☆☆☆☆
☆☆☆☆☆
☆☆☆☆☆

Food & Drinks

Cities
○ ○
○ ○

Memories

OVERALL RATING: /5

Thailand

Dates
Arrive	Depart

Sights
☆☆☆☆☆
☆☆☆☆☆
☆☆☆☆☆
☆☆☆☆☆

Food & Drinks

Cities
○
○
○
○

Memories

OVERALL RATING: /5

Timor-Leste

Dates
Arrive Depart

Sights
☆☆☆☆☆
☆☆☆☆☆
☆☆☆☆☆
☆☆☆☆☆

Food & Drinks

Cities
○   ○
○   ○

Memories

OVERALL RATING: /5

Turkey

Dates
Arrive | Depart

Sights
☆☆☆☆☆
☆☆☆☆☆
☆☆☆☆☆
☆☆☆☆☆

Cities
○   ○
○   ○

Food & Drinks

Memories

OVERALL RATING: /5

Turkmenistan

Dates
Arrive | Depart

Sights
☆☆☆☆☆
☆☆☆☆☆
☆☆☆☆☆
☆☆☆☆☆

Food & Drinks

Cities
○   ○
○   ○

Memories

OVERALL RATING: /5

United Arab Emirates

Dates
Arrive | Depart

Sights
☆☆☆☆☆
☆☆☆☆☆
☆☆☆☆☆
☆☆☆☆☆

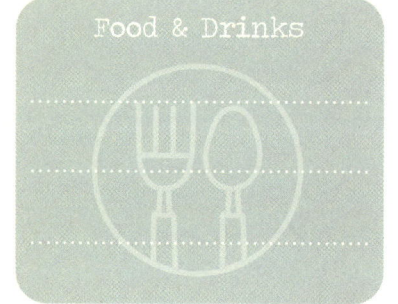

Cities
○ ○
○ ○

Memories

OVERALL RATING: /5

Uzbekistan

Dates
Arrive | Depart

Sights
☆☆☆☆☆
☆☆☆☆☆
☆☆☆☆☆
☆☆☆☆☆

Food & Drinks

Cities
○   ○
○   ○

Memories

OVERALL RATING: /5

Vietnam

Dates
Arrive | Depart

Food & Drinks

Sights
☆☆☆☆☆
☆☆☆☆☆
☆☆☆☆☆
☆☆☆☆☆

Cities
○ ○
○ ○

Memories

OVERALL RATING: /5

Yemen

Dates
Arrive | Depart

Sights
☆☆☆☆☆
☆☆☆☆☆
☆☆☆☆☆
☆☆☆☆☆

Cities
○　　○
○　　○

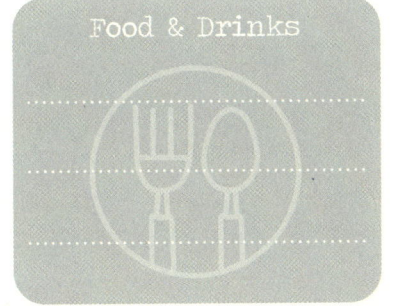
Food & Drinks

Memories

OVERALL RATING: /5

My Favorites

- Market
  - Location
- Tour
  - Location
- Food
  - Location
- I Learned
- Strangest Experience

From ASIA

- Animal
- Location
- Beach
- Location
- Souvenir
- Location
- Must Do
- Funniest Moment

Photos & Keepsakes From...

EUROPE

Draw your best version of the country's flag.

Albania

Dates
Arrive | Depart

Food & Drinks

Sights

List 4 places you visited and rate them by coloring in one to five stars (☆).

☆☆☆☆☆
☆☆☆☆☆
☆☆☆☆☆
☆☆☆☆☆

Cities

○   ○
○   ○

List the cities you explored around the country!

Frame fits a wallet sized photo and don't forget to include a caption below.

Memories

OVERALL RATING: /5

Andorra

Dates
Arrive | Depart

Sights
☆☆☆☆☆
☆☆☆☆☆
☆☆☆☆☆
☆☆☆☆☆

Food & Drinks

Cities
○ ○
○ ○

Memories

OVERALL RATING: /5

Austria

Dates
Arrive | Depart

Sights
☆☆☆☆☆
☆☆☆☆☆
☆☆☆☆☆
☆☆☆☆☆

Cities
○ ○
○ ○

Food & Drinks

Memories

OVERALL RATING: /5

Belarus

Dates
Arrive | Depart

Food & Drinks

Sights
☆☆☆☆☆
☆☆☆☆☆
☆☆☆☆☆
☆☆☆☆☆

Cities
○ ○
○ ○

Memories

OVERALL RATING: /5

Belgium

Dates
Arrive | Depart

Sights
☆☆☆☆☆
☆☆☆☆☆
☆☆☆☆☆
☆☆☆☆☆

Food & Drinks

Cities
○
○
○
○

Memories

OVERALL RATING: /5

Bosnia and Herzegovina

Dates
Arrive | Depart

Sights
☆☆☆☆☆
☆☆☆☆☆
☆☆☆☆☆
☆☆☆☆☆

Food & Drinks

Cities
○ ○
○ ○

Memories

OVERALL RATING: /5

Bulgaria

Dates
Arrive | Depart

Food & Drinks
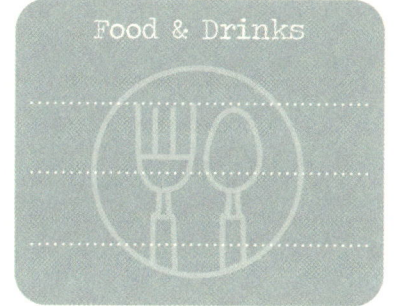

Sights
☆☆☆☆☆
☆☆☆☆☆
☆☆☆☆☆
☆☆☆☆☆

Cities
○　　　○
○　　　○

Memories

OVERALL RATING:　/5

Croatia

Dates
Arrive	Depart

Sights
☆☆☆☆☆
☆☆☆☆☆
☆☆☆☆☆
☆☆☆☆☆

Food & Drinks

Cities
○   ○
○   ○

Memories

OVERALL RATING: /5

Czech Republic

Dates
Arrive | Depart

Sights
☆☆☆☆☆
☆☆☆☆☆
☆☆☆☆☆
☆☆☆☆☆

Food & Drinks

Cities
○　　　○
○　　　○

Memories

OVERALL RATING: /5

Denmark

Dates
Arrive | Depart

Sights
☆☆☆☆☆
☆☆☆☆☆
☆☆☆☆☆
☆☆☆☆☆

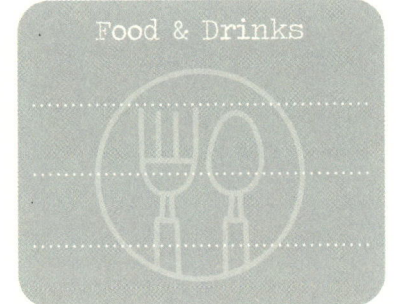

Cities
○   ○
○   ○

Memories

OVERALL RATING: /5

England

Dates
Arrive | Depart

Sights
☆☆☆☆☆
☆☆☆☆☆
☆☆☆☆☆
☆☆☆☆☆

Cities
○   ○
○   ○

Food & Drinks

Memories

OVERALL RATING: /5

Estonia

Dates
Arrive | Depart

Sights
☆☆☆☆☆
☆☆☆☆☆
☆☆☆☆☆
☆☆☆☆☆

Cities
○   ○
○   ○

Memories

OVERALL RATING: /5

Finland

Dates
Arrive | Depart

Sights
☆☆☆☆☆
☆☆☆☆☆
☆☆☆☆☆
☆☆☆☆☆

Food & Drinks

Cities
o   o
o   o

Memories

OVERALL RATING: /5

France

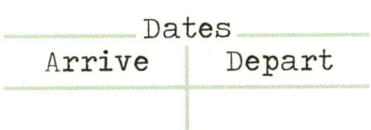

Dates
Arrive | Depart

Sights
☆☆☆☆☆
☆☆☆☆☆
☆☆☆☆☆
☆☆☆☆☆

Cities
○   ○
○   ○

Memories

OVERALL RATING: /5

Germany

Dates
Arrive | Depart

Sights
☆☆☆☆☆
☆☆☆☆☆
☆☆☆☆☆
☆☆☆☆☆

Cities
○ ○
○ ○

Food & Drinks

OVERALL RATING: /5

Memories

Greece

Dates
Arrive | Depart

Food & Drinks

Sights
☆☆☆☆☆
☆☆☆☆☆
☆☆☆☆☆
☆☆☆☆☆

Cities
○ ○
○ ○

Memories

OVERALL RATING: /5

Hungary

Dates
Arrive | Depart

Sights
☆☆☆☆☆
☆☆☆☆☆
☆☆☆☆☆
☆☆☆☆☆

Cities
○　　○
○　　○

Food & Drinks

Memories

OVERALL RATING: /5

Iceland

Dates
Arrive | Depart

Sights
☆☆☆☆☆
☆☆☆☆☆
☆☆☆☆☆
☆☆☆☆☆

Food & Drinks

Cities
○　　○
○　　○

Memories

OVERALL RATING: /5

Northern Ireland

Dates
Arrive	Depart

Food & Drinks

Sights
☆☆☆☆☆
☆☆☆☆☆
☆☆☆☆☆
☆☆☆☆☆

Cities
○   ○
○   ○

Memories

OVERALL RATING: /5

Republic of Ireland

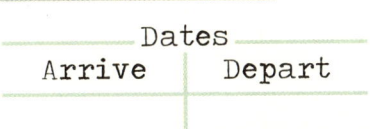

Dates
Arrive | Depart

Sights
☆☆☆☆☆
☆☆☆☆☆
☆☆☆☆☆
☆☆☆☆☆

Food & Drinks

Cities
○   ○
○   ○

Memories

OVERALL RATING: /5

Italy

Dates
Arrive | Depart

Sights
☆☆☆☆☆
☆☆☆☆☆
☆☆☆☆☆
☆☆☆☆☆

Food & Drinks

Cities
○   ○
○   ○

Memories

OVERALL RATING: /5

Kosovo

Dates
Arrive | Depart

Sights
☆☆☆☆☆
☆☆☆☆☆
☆☆☆☆☆
☆☆☆☆☆

Cities
○ ○
○ ○

Memories

OVERALL RATING: /5

Latvia

Dates
Arrive | Depart

Sights
☆☆☆☆☆
☆☆☆☆☆
☆☆☆☆☆
☆☆☆☆☆

Food & Drinks

Cities
○ ○
○ ○

Memories

OVERALL RATING: /5

Liechtenstein

Dates
Arrive | Depart

Sights
☆☆☆☆☆
☆☆☆☆☆
☆☆☆☆☆
☆☆☆☆☆

Food & Drinks

Cities
○ ○
○ ○

Memories

OVERALL RATING: /5

Lithuania

Dates
Arrive | Depart

Sights
☆☆☆☆☆
☆☆☆☆☆
☆☆☆☆☆
☆☆☆☆☆

Cities
○   ○
○   ○

Food & Drinks

Memories

OVERALL RATING: /5

Luxembourg

Dates
| Arrive | Depart |

Sights
☆☆☆☆☆
☆☆☆☆☆
☆☆☆☆☆
☆☆☆☆☆

Food & Drinks

Cities
○　　　○
○　　　○

Memories

OVERALL RATING: /5

Malta

Dates
Arrive | Depart

Food & Drinks

Sights

☆☆☆☆☆
☆☆☆☆☆
☆☆☆☆☆
☆☆☆☆☆

Cities
○   ○
○   ○

Memories

OVERALL RATING: /5

Moldova

Dates
Arrive | Depart

Sights
☆☆☆☆☆
☆☆☆☆☆
☆☆☆☆☆
☆☆☆☆☆

Cities
○ ○
○ ○

Food & Drinks

Memories

OVERALL RATING: /5

Monaco

Dates
Arrive | Depart

Sights
☆☆☆☆☆
☆☆☆☆☆
☆☆☆☆☆
☆☆☆☆☆

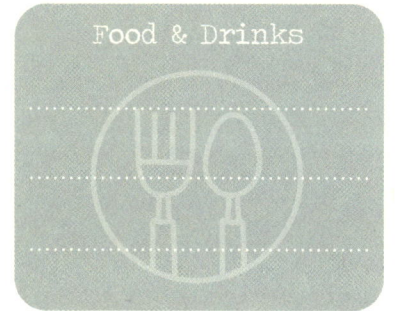
Food & Drinks

Cities
○   ○
○   ○

Memories

OVERALL RATING: /5

Montenegro

Dates
Arrive | Depart

Sights
☆☆☆☆☆
☆☆☆☆☆
☆☆☆☆☆
☆☆☆☆☆

Food & Drinks

Cities
○   ○
○   ○

Memories

OVERALL RATING: /5

Netherlands

Dates
Arrive | Depart

Sights
☆☆☆☆☆
☆☆☆☆☆
☆☆☆☆☆
☆☆☆☆☆

Food & Drinks

Cities
○ ○
○ ○

Memories

OVERALL RATING: /5

North Macedonia

Dates
Arrive | Depart

Sights
☆☆☆☆☆
☆☆☆☆☆
☆☆☆☆☆
☆☆☆☆☆

Food & Drinks

Cities
○ ○
○ ○

Memories

OVERALL RATING: /5

Norway

Dates
Arrive | Depart

Sights
☆☆☆☆☆
☆☆☆☆☆
☆☆☆☆☆
☆☆☆☆☆

Food & Drinks

Cities
○ ○
○ ○

Memories

OVERALL RATING: /5

Poland

Dates
Arrive | Depart

Sights
☆☆☆☆☆
☆☆☆☆☆
☆☆☆☆☆
☆☆☆☆☆

Food & Drinks

Cities
○   ○
○   ○

Memories

OVERALL RATING: /5

Portugal

Dates
Arrive | Depart

Sights
☆☆☆☆☆
☆☆☆☆☆
☆☆☆☆☆
☆☆☆☆☆

Food & Drinks

Cities
○   ○
○   ○

Memories

OVERALL RATING: /5

Romania

Dates
Arrive | Depart

Sights
☆☆☆☆☆
☆☆☆☆☆
☆☆☆☆☆
☆☆☆☆☆

Food & Drinks

Cities
○ ○
○ ○

Memories

OVERALL RATING: /5

San Marino

Dates
Arrive | Depart

Sights
☆☆☆☆☆
☆☆☆☆☆
☆☆☆☆☆
☆☆☆☆☆

Food & Drinks

Cities
○ ○
○ ○

Memories

OVERALL RATING: /5

Scotland

Dates
Arrive	Depart

Sights
☆☆☆☆☆
☆☆☆☆☆
☆☆☆☆☆
☆☆☆☆☆

Food & Drinks

Cities
○ ○
○ ○

Memories

OVERALL RATING: /5

Serbia

Dates
Arrive | Depart

Sights
☆☆☆☆☆
☆☆☆☆☆
☆☆☆☆☆
☆☆☆☆☆

Food & Drinks

Cities
○　　　○
○　　　○

Memories

OVERALL RATING: /5

Slovakia

Dates
Arrive | Depart

Sights
☆☆☆☆☆
☆☆☆☆☆
☆☆☆☆☆
☆☆☆☆☆

Food & Drinks

Cities
○   ○
○   ○

Memories

OVERALL RATING: /5

Slovenia

Dates
| Arrive | Depart |

Sights
☆☆☆☆☆
☆☆☆☆☆
☆☆☆☆☆
☆☆☆☆☆

Food & Drinks

Cities
○   ○
○   ○

Memories

OVERALL RATING: /5

Spain

Dates
Arrive | Depart

Sights
☆☆☆☆☆
☆☆☆☆☆
☆☆☆☆☆
☆☆☆☆☆

Cities
○   ○
○   ○

Memories

OVERALL RATING: /5

Sweden

Dates
Arrive | Depart

Sights
☆☆☆☆☆
☆☆☆☆☆
☆☆☆☆☆
☆☆☆☆☆

Food & Drinks

Cities
○ ○
○ ○

Memories

OVERALL RATING: /5

Switzerland

Dates
Arrive | Depart

Sights
☆☆☆☆☆
☆☆☆☆☆
☆☆☆☆☆
☆☆☆☆☆

Food & Drinks

Cities
○ ○
○ ○

Memories

OVERALL RATING: /5

Ukraine

Dates
Arrive | Depart

Sights
☆☆☆☆☆
☆☆☆☆☆
☆☆☆☆☆
☆☆☆☆☆

Food & Drinks

Cities
○ ○
○ ○

Memories

OVERALL RATING: /5

Vatican City

Dates
Arrive	Depart

Sights
☆☆☆☆☆
☆☆☆☆☆
☆☆☆☆☆
☆☆☆☆☆
☆☆☆☆☆
☆☆☆☆☆
☆☆☆☆☆

Food & Drinks

Memories

OVERALL RATING: /5

Wales

Dates
Arrive | Depart

Sights
☆☆☆☆☆
☆☆☆☆☆
☆☆☆☆☆
☆☆☆☆☆

Food & Drinks

Cities
○   ○
○   ○

Memories

OVERALL RATING: /5

Dates

Arrive | **Depart**

Sights
☆☆☆☆☆
☆☆☆☆☆
☆☆☆☆☆
☆☆☆☆☆

Food & Drinks

Cities
○　　　○
○　　　○

Memories

OVERALL RATING: /5

My Favorites

- Market Location
- Tour Location
- Food Location
- I Learned
- Strangest Experience

From EUROPE

- Animal
- Location
- Beach
- Location
- Souvenir
- Location
- Must Do
- Funniest Moment

Photos & Keepsakes From...

NORTH AMERICA

Draw your best version of the country's flag.

Antigua and Barbuda

List 4 places you visited and rate them by coloring in one to five stars (☆).

Dates
Arrive | Depart

Sights
☆☆☆☆☆
☆☆☆☆☆
☆☆☆☆☆
☆☆☆☆☆

Food & Drinks

Cities
○　　　○
○　　　○

List the cities you explored around the country!

Frame fits a wallet sized photo and don't forget to include a caption below.

Memories

OVERALL RATING: /5

The Bahamas

Dates
Arrive | Depart

Sights
☆☆☆☆☆
☆☆☆☆☆
☆☆☆☆☆
☆☆☆☆☆

Food & Drinks

Cities
○ ○
○ ○

Memories

OVERALL RATING: /5

Barbados

Dates
Arrive	Depart

Sights
☆☆☆☆☆
☆☆☆☆☆
☆☆☆☆☆
☆☆☆☆☆

Food & Drinks

Cities
○   ○
○   ○

Memories

OVERALL RATING: /5

Belize

Dates
Arrive	Depart

Food & Drinks

Sights
☆☆☆☆☆
☆☆☆☆☆
☆☆☆☆☆
☆☆☆☆☆

Cities
○   ○
○   ○

Memories

OVERALL RATING: /5

Canada

Dates
Arrive | Depart

Food & Drinks

Sights
☆☆☆☆☆
☆☆☆☆☆
☆☆☆☆☆
☆☆☆☆☆

Cities
○　　　○
○　　　○

Memories

OVERALL RATING: /5

Costa Rica

Dates
Arrive	Depart

Sights
☆☆☆☆☆
☆☆☆☆☆
☆☆☆☆☆
☆☆☆☆☆

Cities
○　　　○
○　　　○

Memories

OVERALL RATING: /5

Cuba

Dates
Arrive | Depart

Food & Drinks

Sights
☆☆☆☆☆
☆☆☆☆☆
☆☆☆☆☆
☆☆☆☆☆

Cities
○　　　○
○　　　○

Memories

OVERALL RATING: /5

Dominica

Dates
Arrive | Depart

Sights
☆☆☆☆☆
☆☆☆☆☆
☆☆☆☆☆
☆☆☆☆☆

Food & Drinks

Cities
○ ○
○ ○

Memories

OVERALL RATING: /5

Dominican Republic

Dates
Arrive | Depart

Sights
☆☆☆☆☆
☆☆☆☆☆
☆☆☆☆☆
☆☆☆☆☆

Cities
○　　○
○　　○

Food & Drinks

Memories

OVERALL RATING: /5

El Salvador

Dates
Arrive | Depart

Sights
☆☆☆☆☆
☆☆☆☆☆
☆☆☆☆☆
☆☆☆☆☆

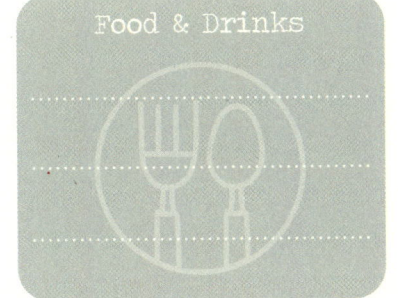
Food & Drinks

Cities
○ ○
○ ○

Memories

OVERALL RATING: /5

Grenada

Dates
Arrive | Depart

Sights
☆☆☆☆☆
☆☆☆☆☆
☆☆☆☆☆
☆☆☆☆☆

Food & Drinks

Cities
○   ○
○   ○

Memories

OVERALL RATING: /5

Guatemala

Dates
Arrive | Depart

Sights
☆☆☆☆☆
☆☆☆☆☆
☆☆☆☆☆
☆☆☆☆☆

Food & Drinks

Cities
○   ○
○   ○

Memories

OVERALL RATING: /5

Haiti

Dates
Arrive | Depart

Sights
☆☆☆☆☆
☆☆☆☆☆
☆☆☆☆☆
☆☆☆☆☆

Food & Drinks

Cities
○   ○
○   ○

Memories

OVERALL RATING: /5

Honduras

Dates
Arrive | Depart

Sights
☆☆☆☆☆
☆☆☆☆☆
☆☆☆☆☆
☆☆☆☆☆

Cities
○ ○
○ ○

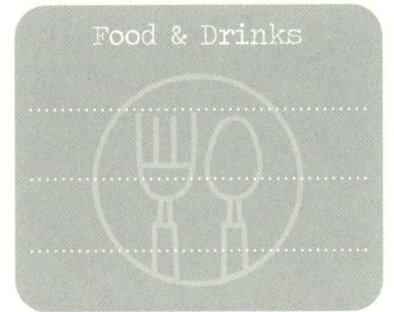
Food & Drinks

Memories

OVERALL RATING: /5

Jamaica

Dates
Arrive	Depart

Food & Drinks

Sights
☆☆☆☆☆
☆☆☆☆☆
☆☆☆☆☆
☆☆☆☆☆

Cities
- ○
- ○
- ○
- ○

Memories

OVERALL RATING: /5

Mexico

Dates
Arrive | Depart

Sights
☆☆☆☆☆
☆☆☆☆☆
☆☆☆☆☆
☆☆☆☆☆

Food & Drinks

Cities
○ ○
○ ○

Memories

OVERALL RATING: /5

Nicaragua

Dates
Arrive | Depart

Sights
☆☆☆☆☆
☆☆☆☆☆
☆☆☆☆☆
☆☆☆☆☆

Food & Drinks

Cities
○ ○
○ ○

Memories

OVERALL RATING: /5

Panama

Dates
Arrive | Depart

Sights
☆☆☆☆☆
☆☆☆☆☆
☆☆☆☆☆
☆☆☆☆☆

Food & Drinks

Cities
○ ○
○ ○

Memories

OVERALL RATING: /5

Saint Kitts and Nevis

Dates
Arrive | Depart

Sights

Food & Drinks

Cities
○　　　○
○　　　○

Memories

OVERALL RATING: /5

Saint Lucia

Dates
Arrive | Depart

Sights
☆☆☆☆☆
☆☆☆☆☆
☆☆☆☆☆
☆☆☆☆☆

Food & Drinks

Cities
○   ○
○   ○

Memories

OVERALL RATING: /5

Saint Vincent and the Grenadines

Dates
Arrive | Depart

Sights
☆☆☆☆☆
☆☆☆☆☆
☆☆☆☆☆
☆☆☆☆☆

Food & Drinks

Cities
○   ○
○   ○

Memories

OVERALL RATING: /5

Trinidad and Tobago

Dates
Arrive | Depart

Sights
☆☆☆☆☆
☆☆☆☆☆
☆☆☆☆☆
☆☆☆☆☆

Cities
○ ○
○ ○

Food & Drinks

Memories

OVERALL RATING: /5

United States of America

Dates
Arrive | Depart

Sights
☆☆☆☆☆
☆☆☆☆☆
☆☆☆☆☆
☆☆☆☆☆

Food & Drinks

Cities
○   ○
○   ○

Memories

OVERALL RATING: /5

Dates

Arrive | Depart

Food & Drinks

Sights

☆☆☆☆☆
☆☆☆☆☆
☆☆☆☆☆
☆☆☆☆☆

Cities

○
○
○
○

Memories

OVERALL RATING: /5

My Favorites

- Market
  - Location
- Tour
  - Location
- Food
  - Location
- I Learned
- Strangest Experience

- Animal
- Location
- Beach
- Souvenir
- Location
- Location
- Location

From NORTH AMERICA

- Must Do
- Funniest Moment

Photos & Keepsakes From...

OCEANIA

Draw your best version of the country's flag.

Australia

List 4 places you visited and rate them by coloring in one to five stars (☆).

Dates
Arrive | Depart

Sights

☆☆☆☆☆
☆☆☆☆☆
☆☆☆☆☆
☆☆☆☆☆

Food & Drinks

Cities

○   ○
○   ○

List the cities you explored around the country!

Frame fits a wallet sized photo and don't forget to include a caption below.

Memories

OVERALL RATING: /5

Fiji

Dates
Arrive | Depart

Sights
☆☆☆☆☆
☆☆☆☆☆
☆☆☆☆☆
☆☆☆☆☆

Food & Drinks

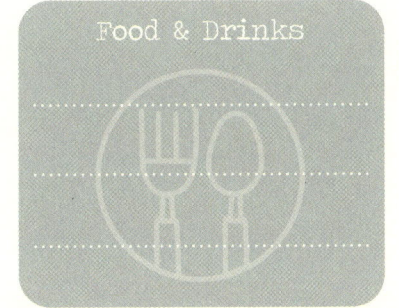

Cities
○ ○
○ ○

Memories

OVERALL RATING: /5

Kiribati

Dates
Arrive   Depart

Sights
☆☆☆☆☆
☆☆☆☆☆
☆☆☆☆☆
☆☆☆☆☆

Cities
○   ○
○   ○

Food & Drinks

Memories

OVERALL RATING: /5

Marshall Islands

Dates
Arrive | Depart

Sights
☆☆☆☆☆
☆☆☆☆☆
☆☆☆☆☆
☆☆☆☆☆

Food & Drinks

Cities
○ ○
○ ○

Memories

OVERALL RATING: /5

Federated States of Micronesia

Dates
Arrive | Depart

Sights
☆☆☆☆☆
☆☆☆☆☆
☆☆☆☆☆
☆☆☆☆☆

Food & Drinks

Cities
○　　　○
○　　　○

Memories

OVERALL RATING: /5

Nauru

Dates
Arrive | Depart

Sights
☆☆☆☆☆
☆☆☆☆☆
☆☆☆☆☆
☆☆☆☆☆

Food & Drinks

Cities
○　　○
○　　○

Memories

OVERALL RATING: /5

New Zealand

Dates
Arrive | Depart

Food & Drinks

Sights
☆☆☆☆☆
☆☆☆☆☆
☆☆☆☆☆
☆☆☆☆☆

Cities
○   ○
○   ○

Memories

OVERALL RATING: /5

Palau

Dates
Arrive	Depart

Sights
☆☆☆☆☆
☆☆☆☆☆
☆☆☆☆☆
☆☆☆☆☆

Food & Drinks

Cities
-
-
-
-

Memories

OVERALL RATING: /5

Papua New Guinea

Dates
Arrive | Depart

Food & Drinks

Sights
☆☆☆☆☆
☆☆☆☆☆
☆☆☆☆☆
☆☆☆☆☆

Cities

Memories

OVERALL RATING: /5

Samoa

Dates
Arrive | Depart

Sights
☆☆☆☆☆
☆☆☆☆☆
☆☆☆☆☆
☆☆☆☆☆

Cities
○　　○
○　　○

Food & Drinks

Memories

OVERALL RATING: /5

Solomon Islands

Dates
Arrive | Depart

Sights
☆☆☆☆☆
☆☆☆☆☆
☆☆☆☆☆
☆☆☆☆☆

Food & Drinks

Cities
○　　○
○　　○

Memories

OVERALL RATING: /5

Tonga

Dates
Arrive | Depart

Sights
☆☆☆☆☆
☆☆☆☆☆
☆☆☆☆☆
☆☆☆☆☆

Food & Drinks

Cities
○ ○
○ ○

Memories

OVERALL RATING: /5

Tuvalu

Dates
Arrive | Depart

Sights
☆☆☆☆☆
☆☆☆☆☆
☆☆☆☆☆
☆☆☆☆☆

Food & Drinks

Cities
○   ○
○   ○

Memories

OVERALL RATING: /5

Vanuatu

Dates
Arrive | Depart

Sights
☆☆☆☆☆
☆☆☆☆☆
☆☆☆☆☆
☆☆☆☆☆

Food & Drinks

Cities
○ ○
○ ○

Memories

OVERALL RATING: /5

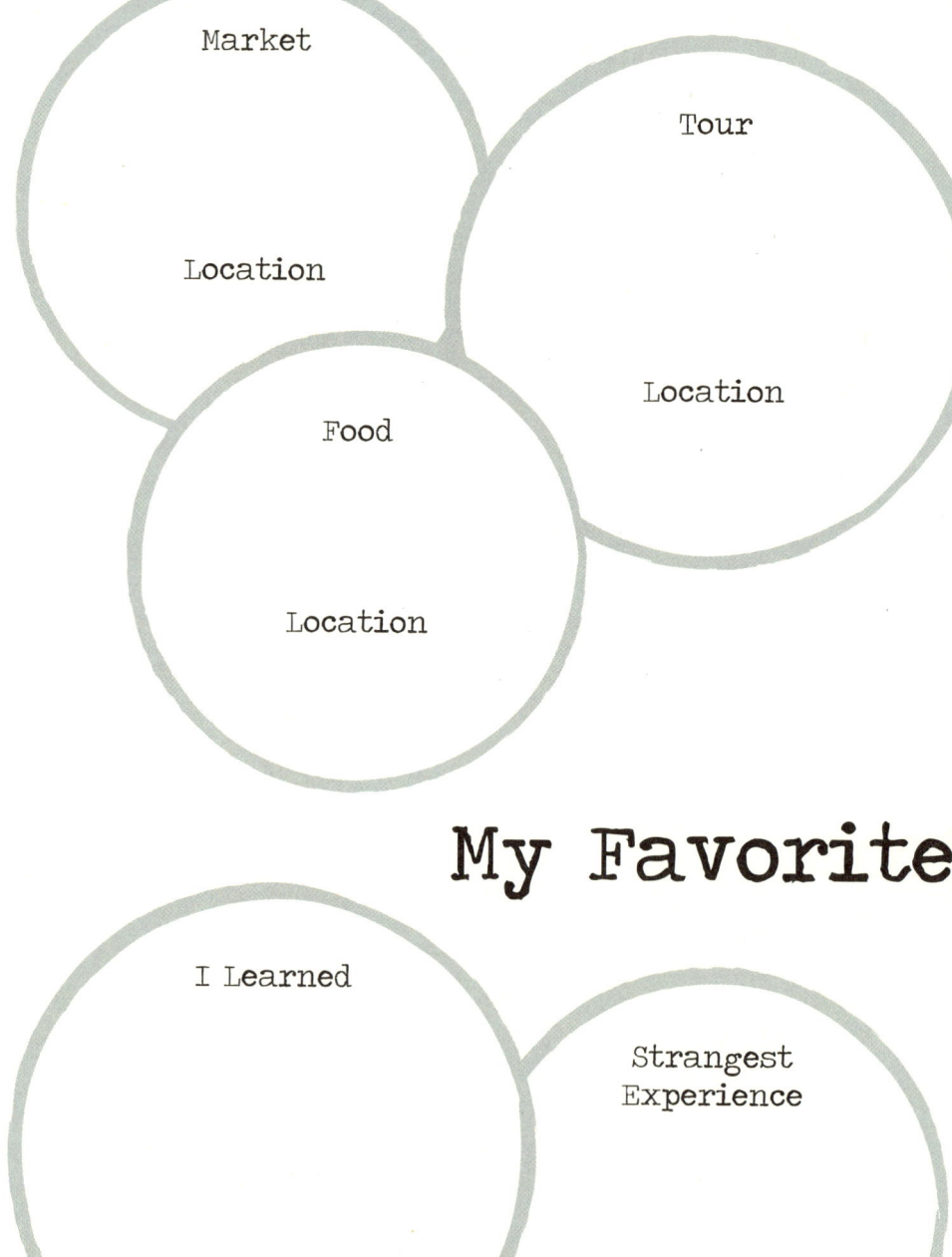

From OCEANIA

- Animal
- Location
- Beach
- Souvenir
- Location
- Location
- Must Do
- Funniest Moment

Photos & Keepsakes From...

Draw your best version of the country's flag.

Argentina

List 4 places you visited and rate them by coloring in one to five stars (☆).

Dates
Arrive | Depart

Sights
☆☆☆☆☆
☆☆☆☆☆
☆☆☆☆☆
☆☆☆☆☆

Food & Drinks

Cities
○　　　○
○　　　○

List the cities you explored around the country!

Frame fits a wallet sized photo and don't forget to include a caption below.

Memories

OVERALL RATING: /5

Bolivia

Dates
Arrive | Depart

Sights
☆☆☆☆☆
☆☆☆☆☆
☆☆☆☆☆
☆☆☆☆☆

Food & Drinks

Cities
○　　　○
○　　　○

Memories

OVERALL RATING: /5

Brazil

Dates
Arrive	Depart

Sights
☆☆☆☆☆
☆☆☆☆☆
☆☆☆☆☆
☆☆☆☆☆

Food & Drinks

Cities
○ ○
○ ○

Memories

OVERALL RATING: /5

Chile

Dates
Arrive | Depart

Sights
☆☆☆☆☆
☆☆☆☆☆
☆☆☆☆☆
☆☆☆☆☆

Food & Drinks

Cities
○
○
○
○

Memories

OVERALL RATING: /5

Colombia

Dates
Arrive | Depart

Sights
☆☆☆☆☆
☆☆☆☆☆
☆☆☆☆☆
☆☆☆☆☆

Food & Drinks

Cities
○   ○
○   ○

Memories

OVERALL RATING: /5

Ecuador

Dates
Arrive | Depart

Sights
☆☆☆☆☆
☆☆☆☆☆
☆☆☆☆☆
☆☆☆☆☆

Food & Drinks

Cities
○   ○
○   ○

Memories

OVERALL RATING: /5

Guyana

Dates
Arrive | Depart

Sights
☆☆☆☆☆
☆☆☆☆☆
☆☆☆☆☆
☆☆☆☆☆

Food & Drinks

Cities
○   ○
○   ○

Memories

OVERALL RATING: /5

Paraguay

Dates
Arrive | Depart

Sights
☆☆☆☆☆
☆☆☆☆☆
☆☆☆☆☆
☆☆☆☆☆

Food & Drinks

Cities
○   ○
○   ○

Memories

OVERALL RATING: /5

Peru

Dates
Arrive | Depart

Sights
☆☆☆☆☆
☆☆☆☆☆
☆☆☆☆☆
☆☆☆☆☆

Food & Drinks

Cities
○　　　○
○　　　○

Memories

OVERALL RATING: /5

Suriname

Dates
Arrive | Depart

Sights
☆☆☆☆☆
☆☆☆☆☆
☆☆☆☆☆
☆☆☆☆☆

Cities
○ ○
○ ○

Memories

OVERALL RATING: /5

Uruguay

Dates
Arrive | Depart

Sights
☆☆☆☆☆
☆☆☆☆☆
☆☆☆☆☆
☆☆☆☆☆

Food & Drinks

Cities
○   ○
○   ○

Memories

OVERALL RATING: /5

Venezuela

Dates
Arrive | Depart

Sights
☆☆☆☆☆
☆☆☆☆☆
☆☆☆☆☆
☆☆☆☆☆

Food & Drinks

Cities
○   ○
○   ○

Memories

OVERALL RATING: /5

From SOUTH AMERICA

- Animal
- Location
- Beach
- Souvenir
- Location
- Location
- Must Do
- Funniest Moment

Draw your best version of the flag.

Antarctica

Dates
Arrive | Depart

Sights
List 4 places you visited and rate them by coloring in one to five stars (☆).

☆☆☆☆☆
☆☆☆☆☆
☆☆☆☆☆
☆☆☆☆☆

Stations
○　　　　○
○　　　　○

List the stations you explored!

Frame fits a wallet sized photo and don't forget to include a caption below.

Memories

OVERALL RATING: /5

Dates
Arrive | Depart

Food & Drinks

Sights
☆☆☆☆☆
☆☆☆☆☆
☆☆☆☆☆
☆☆☆☆☆

Cities
○ ○
○ ○

Memories

OVERALL RATING: /5

Dates
Arrive | Depart

Food & Drinks

Sights
☆☆☆☆☆
☆☆☆☆☆
☆☆☆☆☆
☆☆☆☆☆

Cities
○
○
○
○

Memories

OVERALL RATING: /5

Sometimes you just need a blank slate to do you!

Hello from Around the

Bonjour FROM *France*

FROM _____   FROM _____
FROM _____   FROM _____
FROM _____   FROM _____
FROM _____   FROM _____
FROM _____   FROM _____
FROM _____   FROM _____
FROM _____   FROM _____
FROM _____   FROM _____
FROM _____   FROM _____
FROM _____   FROM _____
FROM _____   FROM _____
FROM _____   FROM _____
FROM _____   FROM _____
FROM _____   FROM _____
FROM _____   FROM _____
FROM _____   FROM _____
FROM _____   FROM _____
FROM _____   FROM _____
FROM _____   FROM _____
FROM _____   FROM _____
FROM _____   FROM _____
FROM _____   FROM _____

Travel Library

Fill these shelves with the titles you read on the road.

The Wonders of the World

- ☐ Christ the Redeemer
- ☐ Pyramid of Giza
- ☐ The Colosseum
- ☐ Petra

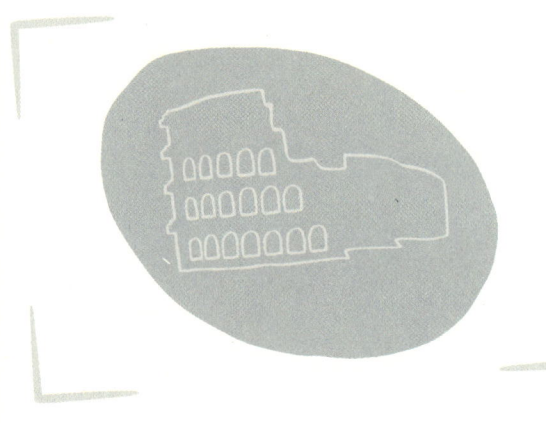

Snap a photo with each of the Wonders and collect them here!

- ☐ Great Wall of China
- ☐ Chichén Itzá
- ☐ Machu Picchu
- ☐ Taj Mahal

New Places,

Story:

Where We Met:

Name:

Story:

Where We Met:

Name:

Story:

Where We Met:

Name:

Remember new friends you meet along

Story:

Where We Met:

Name:

Story:

Where We Met:

Name:

Story:

Where We Met:

Name:

Bring New Faces

Story:

Name:

Where We Met:

Story:

Where We Met:

Name:

Story:

Name:

Where We Met:

Name:

...he way, by recording their VIP details.

Story:

Name:

Where We Met:

Story:

Where We Met:

Story:

Name:

Where We Met:

Name:

Choose an item and collect one from each country you visit. Stick it on work, candy wrappers, matchbook covers, stickers, newspaper clippings, fabric swatches, ink stamps, anything cats, pressed pennies, key cards, coasters, or bottle labels.

this page and watch your collection grow, along with the variety. Here are some ideas: postage stamps, dried flowers or leaves, tea bags, postcards, menus, maps, patches, business cards, vintage photographs, bookmarks, string bracelets, art

Money, Money, Money!

Trace each new coin you find, and watch the money roll in!

Just the Ticket!

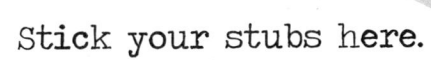

Stick your stubs here.

To Sum Up My Adventures...